MW01232184

LEADING ACROSS GENERATIONS

A Practical Guide for Managing and Motivating
a MultiGenerational Workforce

Jeff Arnold

This writing is a primer for Leading Across Generations.

Managing a Motivating a Multi-generational Workforce

primer noun (i)

prim*er, chiefly British

'pri-me\

Definition (entries): a small introductory book on a subject: a short informative piece of writing

It remains my earnest aim that all who read these pages feel my sincere enthusiasm for Leading, Developing, Managing, and Encouraging Tomorrow's Leaders.

Your Generational Birth Sequence Matters Not,

The Future is Yours. Lead **BOLDY**

TABLE OF CONTENTS

Each of the following chapters will provide a deep dive into multi-generational leadership challenges and provide real world examples and anecdotes.

Additionally, I have curated a Leaders Tip Sheets for Difficult Conversations using the QR Code below.

WHAT'S THIS PRIMER ABOUT:

As an executive with a career spanning prominent, small businesses, startup companies, hyper-growth, debt-funded unicorns, VC-backed, and private equity-partnered firms, I have encountered many leadership challenges, including managing teams that include members from various generations.

Admittedly, leading such teams requires a unique set of skills and strategies.

In this short primer I use a simple approach to attempt at recognizing each generation's different communication styles and preferences.

These examples below may seem a bit stereotypical, but I submit to you that:

", Baby Boomers may prefer face-to-face conversations and formal memos, while Millennials prefer quick text messages and informal chats."

Another Assumption For Instance:

"Gen X may place a higher value on loyalty, stability & employer commitment, while Gen Z may prioritize working with a firm committed to social impact."

Through Three Decades of experience, I have learned that managing across generations can be challenging but highly rewarding.

When we as leaders learn to leverage the strengths and perspectives of each generation, we are then able to create more innovative and dynamic teams.

Indeed, your skillset is going to be stretched and you will be placed in very uncomfortable emotionally vulnerable territory, but isn't that where all the best growth happens ?

I hope you enjoy reading this short primer as much as I enjoyed writing it.

PROLOGUE:

As you read this book, take a moment to appreciate the diversity around you.

Look to your left, and you might see a Baby Boomer staring at you with a hard work ethic.

To your right, a Gen Xer wonders why you're not working harder.

Behind you, a Millennial is probably texting on their phone.

In front of you, a Gen Zer is scrolling through TikTok.

And lest we forget the newest workforce additions possibly accompanying you or working around your home office, Gen Alpha, who are likely adding up more daily screen time than you.

Don't let these generational differences scare you! This book will take you on a journey through the past, present, and future of the multi-generational Workplace, with insights and strategies for managing teams, creating cultures of inclusion, and preparing for a lot of work.

Briefly, in this succinct primer, purposefully "Twitterized" with short paragraphs and small chapter layouts, You'll learn that each generation has its unique strengths and challenges and how to leverage these differences to create a culture of collaboration and innovation.

Join me as we learn from the hardworking Baby Boomers to the tech-savvy Gen-Zers; there's something to learn from each generation.

Get Comfy, silence your phone, sit back, and get ready to laugh and learn as we explore the fascinating world of the multi-generational Workplace. Whether you're a seasoned executive, a new manager, or someone trying to navigate the complexities of the modern Workplace, this primer is for you!

Jeff Arnold

Chapter 1:

AN INTRODUCTION TO THE GENERATIONS

Generational differences have been a topic of interest and discussion for decades, particularly as they relate to the Workplace.

Understanding the characteristics and values of different generations can foster better communication and collaboration and can lead to a more productive and harmonious work environment.

In this primer, we will introduce the five major living generations and discuss common stereotypes and misconceptions associated with each.

Subsequent chapters will take a deeper dive into each generation.

Generation	Birth Year	Age in 2023
Baby Boomers	1946-64	59-77 years old
Generation X	1965-1980	43-58 years old
Millennials	1981-1996	27-42 years old
Generation Y (or Gen Z)	1997-2012	11-26 years old
Generation Alpha	2013-2025	0-10 years old
Note: The birth years for each generation can vary slightly depending on the source, so there may be some overlap between generations. Also, some people may indetify with a different generation than the one they were born into based on their expereinces and cultural influences.		

Baby Boomers | Boomer

The first generation we will examine is the Baby Boomers, born between 1946 and 1964. This generation is known for its size and influence, as they were born during a time of economic prosperity and social change.

Baby Boomers are hardworking, competitive, and optimistic and value loyalty and stability in the Workplace.

They are also often associated with traditional gender roles and a focus on work over personal life.

While these stereotypes may be true for some Baby Boomers, it's essential to recognize that individuals within this generation are diverse and may not fit into these generalizations.

Generation X (GENX)

Generation X was born between 1965 and 1980. Often referred to as the "latchkey kids," this generation grew up during a time of economic downturn and social upheaval, which may have contributed to their independent and self-sufficient nature.

Generation X is often characterized as cynical, adaptable, and entrepreneurial, and they value work-life balance and flexibility in the Workplace.

They are also often associated with a lack of loyalty and a tendency to job-hop. But, again, it's essential to recognize that these are generalizations and are not valid for every generation member.

Millenials | Techies

Millennials, born between 1981 and 1996, are the largest generation in the Workforce today.

They are known for their technological savvy, global mindset, and desire for social change.

Millennials value work-life balance and meaningful work, and they often seek opportunities for growth and development in their careers.

They are often characterized as entitled, self-centered, and easily distracted. Still, these stereotypes may be more a reflection of societal changes and technological advancements than the characteristics of the generation itself.

Generation Y: Socially Conscious

Generation Y, also known as Gen Z, is the youngest generation in the Workforce today, born between 1997 and 2012.

This generation is tech-savvy, diverse, and socially conscious.

They value authenticity and transparency in the Workplace and are often interested in entrepreneurship and side hustles.

However, because they are still relatively new to the Workforce, less research is available on their characteristics and values.

Generation Alpha: On Their Way

Finally, Generation Alpha is the youngest generation, born from 2013 to 2025.

While they are not yet part of the Workforce, it must be noted they will enter it in the coming years and bring their unique characteristics and values.

This generation is expected to be even more tech-savvy and global-minded than their predecessors, with a focus on innovation and creativity.

Generational Summary

It's important to recognize that these generalizations are not absolute and that individuals within each generation may not fit into these categories.

However, understanding some of each generation's common characteristics and values can help foster better communication and collaboration in the Workplace.

It's also important to recognize that various factors, including societal changes, technological advancements, and economic conditions, shape each generation's experiences and values.

One of the most common stereotypes associated with generational differences is that older generations are resistant to change and younger generations are entitled and easily distracted.

However, research has shown that these stereotypes are only sometimes true. For example, a study conducted by the Pew Research Center found that Baby Boomers and Generation Xers were just as likely as Millennials to embrace new technology and social media.

Similarly, a study conducted by the Harvard Business Review found that older workers were just as motivated and engaged in their work as younger workers and often had a greater sense of loyalty to their employers.

Another misconception is that generational differences are a significant source of conflict in the Workplace. While it's true that different generations may have different values and communication styles, research has shown that age diversity in the Workplace can lead to better problem-solving and decision-making.

When teams are uniquely made up of individuals from different generations, they are more likely to bring different perspectives and ideas to the table, leading to more innovative solutions.

Understanding generational differences can also be helpful when it comes to recruitment and retention.

Each generation has its own values and priorities regarding work, and employers who recognize and accommodate these differences are more likely to attract and retain top talent.

For example, Millennials and Generation Z are often attracted to companies with vital social and environmental missions, while Baby Boomers and Generation X may value job security and stability more.

To effectively manage and work with individuals from different generations, it's important to focus on individual differences rather than generational stereotypes.

While it's helpful to be aware of some common characteristics and values of different generations, remember to recognize that each person is unique and may not fit neatly into a particular generational category.

It's also important to recognize that individuals within each generation may have different experiences and values based on factors such as race, gender, and socioeconomic status.

As we shift from this chapter to the next, your key takeaway from this section is that understanding generational differences can be helpful when it comes to fostering better communication and collaboration in the Workplace.

A stereotypical assumption made by leaders and applied with a broad brush to each generation's stereotypes is certain to be met with peril.

By focusing on individual differences and recognizing the factors that shape each person's experiences and values, leaders and employers can create a more inclusive and productive work environment for each generation.

Chapter 2:

BABY BOOMERS

The Impact of Baby Boomers on the Workplace

Baby Boomers, born between 1946 and 1964, have significantly impacted the Workplace. As the largest generation, they have influenced everything from work culture to consumer behavior. Despite facing retirement age, many Baby Boomers continue to work and contribute to the Workforce. Understanding their values and work ethic is crucial for any organization leveraging its knowledge and experience.

Boomers grew up during a time of prosperity and optimism in the United States. They were raised with the belief that hard work and determination could lead to success. This mindset has translated into a strong work ethic and a focus on career success for many Baby Boomers. They are often characterized as dedicated and loyal employees committed to their employers and willing to work long hours to achieve their goals.

Discussion of Baby Boomers' Work Ethics and Values

On the subject matter of Work Ethics and Values, Baby Boomers tend to prioritize financial stability and security. Many of them came of age during a time of economic prosperity but also lived through periods of recession and economic downturn. As a result, they tend to be more cautious with their finances and place a high value on job security and stability. They also tend to value traditional career paths and may be more likely to stay with a single employer for many years.

Addressing challenges such as retirement and succession planning

One challenge facing Baby Boomers in the Workplace is retirement.

As this generation ages, many are reaching retirement age and may be considering leaving the Workforce. However, many Baby Boomers choose to work longer for financial reasons or because they enjoy their jobs and want to stay engaged. Admittedly, this can create challenges for employers who need to plan for succession and ensure that younger employees have opportunities for advancement.

Another challenge is ensuring that Baby Boomers' knowledge and experience are leveraged effectively. With decades of experience in the Workforce, Baby Boomers have a wealth of knowledge and expertise to offer. However, it can be difficult for younger employees to learn from and work alongside older colleagues.

To lead across generations, leaders and employers can address this by implementing mentorship programs and providing opportunities for Baby Boomers to share their knowledge and experience with younger employees.

One way to leverage Baby Boomers' knowledge and experience is through flexible retirement options. Instead of simply retiring outright, many Baby Boomers may be interested in transitioning to part-time or consulting roles. This can allow them to continue working and contributing to the organization while providing opportunities for younger employees to take on more responsibilities and develop their skills.

Succession planning is another essential consideration when managing Baby Boomers in the Workforce. As older employees retire or transition to new roles, it's vital to ensure that there are younger employees who are ready and able to step into their shoes. This requires careful planning and development of younger employees to ensure they have the skills and experience to succeed in more senior roles.

How to Leverage Baby Boomers' Knowledge and Experience

Employers must create a culture of respect and inclusivity to address these challenges and effectively leverage Baby Boomers' knowledge and experience. This implies that leaders value the contributions of all employees, regardless of age or generation, and provide opportunities for individuals of all ages to learn and grow. Employers should also be mindful of older employees' unique challenges and needs, such as healthcare and retirement planning.

Baby Boomers have had a marked and significant impact on the Workplace, and their knowledge and experience can be a valuable asset for organizations.

To be an effective leader, however, employers must be mindful of the challenges associated with an aging workforce, including retirement planning and succession management. By creating a culture of respect and inclusivity and providing opportunities for knowledge sharing and mentorship, employers can effectively leverage Baby Boomers' knowledge and experience while preparing for the future.

"Baby boomers are the pioneers of a generation that paved the way for progress, fought for change, and built a world of endless possibilities."

Jeff Arnold

Chapter 3:

GENERATION X

The Characteristics and values of Generation X

Generation X, born between 1965 and 1980, is often referred to as the "forgotten" generation. Sandwiched between the larger Baby Boomer and Millennial generations, Gen X is often overlooked by many workplace studies and discussions.

This forgotten generation is an important and valuable part of the Workforce, with unique characteristics and values that can benefit any organization.

One defining characteristic of Generation X is their independence and self-reliance. Growing up during economic uncertainty and social change, many Gen Xers learned to fend for themselves and rely on their resources.

This mindset has translated into a strong work ethic and a focus on individual achievement. As a result, Gen Xers are often characterized as hardworking, pragmatic, and adaptable employees.

In terms of values, Gen X prioritizes work-life balance and flexibility.

How to motivate and engage Gen X employees

Unlike Baby Boomers, who often put career success above all else, Gen Xers highly value family and personal time.

Gen X workers are often willing to work hard and put in extra effort to see projects completed on time, under budget, and as promised.

To motivate and engage Gen X employees, it's important to provide opportunities for growth and development.

This generation is known for its entrepreneurial spirit and willingness to take risks, so offering opportunities for innovation and creativity can be a powerful motivator.

Gen Xers also value autonomy and independence, so providing them with the tools and resources they need to succeed can be more effective than micromanagement or close supervision.

It's also important to recognize the impact of historical events on Generation X.

Discussion of the impact of the recession and other historical events

This generation grew up during rapid technological change, including the rise of personal computers and the internet.

They were also profoundly affected by events such as the Cold War, The Challenger Explosion, the fall of the Berlin Wall, multiple economic downturns and the Gulf War. These experiences have shaped their worldview and influenced their work and life approaches.

Balancing Work and Family for Gen X Employees

One challenge facing many Gen X employees is balancing work and family responsibilities. As a result, this generation is often referred to as the "sandwich generation," as many are simultaneously caring for aging parents and raising children.

This "sandwiching" can create stress and strain their personal lives, ultimately affecting their job performance. Employers can address this by offering family-friendly policies, such as paid leave or flexible scheduling, and being understanding of employees' personal needs and responsibilities.

The best way to lead and engage Gen X employees is to provide opportunities for social connection and collaboration. This generation values teamwork and collaboration but may be more reserved in their communication style than Millennials or Gen Z.

Providing opportunities for team-building activities or social events can help foster a sense of community and connectedness among Gen X employees.

Generation X may be a smaller and often overlooked generation, but they are a valuable and crucially significant part of the Workforce.

By understanding their unique characteristics and values, leaders can create a work environment that supports and engages Gen X employees.

Backed by their strong work ethic, entrepreneurial spirit, and focus on work-life balance, Gen Xers have the potential to make significant contributions to any organization.

"Generation X is the resilient and adaptable generation that grew up in the shadow of the past and the uncertainty of the future, yet emerged as the driving force of innovation and transformation."

Chapter 4:

MILLENNIALS

Common Misconceptions about Millennials

Millennials, born between 1981 and 1996, are often scrutinized and criticized in the Workplace. Commonly referred to as the "me" generation, Millennials are frequently stereotyped as entitled, lazy, and self-centered.

Like most stereotypes, these misconceptions are often inaccurate and fail to recognize this generation's unique characteristics and values.

Discussion of the impact of technology on Millennials

One of the defining features of Millennials is their relationship with technology. Unlike previous generations, Millennials grew up with easy access to computers, smartphones, and the internet.

This "forever" access has led to a strong preference for digital communication and a high level of comfort with technology. While this can sometimes lead to distractions in the Workplace, it can also be a valuable asset for companies looking to innovate and stay ahead of the curve.

One common misconception about Millennials is that they are less committed to their jobs than previous generations. In reality, Millennials often seek meaningful work and a sense of purpose in their careers. In addition, they value work-life balance and are willing to make sacrifices to achieve it. This means employers who offer opportunities for personal and professional growth and flexible work arrangements are more likely to attract and retain Millennial employees.

Strategies for Attracting and Retaining Millennial Employees

An argued stance about Millennials is that they are not interested in traditional career paths. While it's true that this generation values flexibility and may be more likely to switch jobs than previous generations, they are still looking for meaningful and challenging work.

Leaders & Employers can attract and retain Millennial employees by offering opportunities for growth and development, such as mentorship programs or leadership training.

One strategy for engaging Millennials is to provide opportunities for social connection and collaboration. This generation values teamwork and collaboration and may be more likely to thrive in a collaborative work environment. Providing opportunities for team-building activities, social events, or open office spaces can help foster a sense of community and connectedness among Millennial employees.

Addressing the desire for work-life balance and purpose-driven work

Another strategy for engaging Millennials is to offer opportunities for purpose-driven work. This generation is often motivated by social and environmental issues and may be more likely to seek out employers who prioritize corporate social responsibility.

Every Leader seeking to connect with this generation should be aware of the desire for work-life balance among Millennial employees. This generation values personal time and may be more likely to prioritize their personal lives over their careers.

"Millennials are the generation of change-makers, disrupting the status quo and challenging the norms, with their unwavering conviction, relentless pursuit of purpose, and fearless determination to create a better world.

Chapter 5:

GENERATION Z

Characteristics of Gen Z and how they differ from Millennials

Generation Z, born between 1997 and 2012, is the newest generation to enter the Workforce and is already making an impact.

Often referred to as "digital natives," Gen Z employees bring a unique set of skills, values, and preferences to the Workplace. To effectively engage and retain Gen Z employees, leaders and employers must understand their characteristics and values and the impact of technology on their communication style.

The impact of technology on Gen Z and their communication Style

One of the key differences between Gen Z and Millennials is their relationship with technology.

While Millennials grew up with technology, Gen Z was born into a world where technology is ubiquitous.

This "birthright" provides Gen Z with a higher level of comfort and familiarity with technology, and they often prefer digital communication over in-person communication.

Employers can leverage this preference by providing opportunities for virtual collaboration, such as video conferencing or virtual team-building activities.

Strategies for Engaging and Retaining Gen Z Employees

Another key characteristic of Gen Z is their desire for diversity and inclusion. This generation is the most racially and ethnically diverse generation in history, often motivated by social justice issues.

Employers prioritizing diversity, equity, and inclusion in their hiring and workplace practices are more likely to attract and retain Gen Z employees.

Additionally, offering opportunities for employee-led diversity and inclusion initiatives can help engage and empower Gen Z employees.

Gen Z employees also tend to value social responsibility and sustainability. They are often motivated by a desire to impact the world positively, and they may seek employers who prioritize environmental and social responsibility.

Employers can engage Gen Z employees by communicating their commitment to sustainability and social responsibility and offering opportunities for employee-led initiatives supporting these values.

In terms of communication style, Gen Z employees tend to prefer short, visual, and interactive forms of communication. In addition, they are accustomed to consuming information through social media and other digital platforms and may have shorter attention spans than previous generations.

Leaders will do well to remember to engage Gen Z employees by providing precise and concise communication, as well as opportunities for interactive and engaging learning experiences.

Addressing the desire for diversity and social responsibility

Gen Z employees are starving for opportunities for growth and development. This generation is often seeking new challenges and opportunities to learn and grow. Employers can offer mentorship programs, leadership training, or other development opportunities to engage and retain Gen Z employees.

This generation has grown up in a world where the lines between work and personal life are often blurred, and they may prioritize personal time and wellness. As a result, offering flexible work arrangements, such as telecommuting or flexible schedules, can be a powerful motivator for Gen Z employees.

 Gen Z employees bring a unique set of skills, values, and preferences to the Workplace. By understanding their characteristics and values, as well as the impact of technology on their communication style, employers can engage and retain Gen Z employees.

*"Generation Z, Digital natives who are rewriting the
rules and reshaping the future, fueled by their boundless
creativity, fearless spirit, and unwavering determination to
make a difference in the world."*

Chapter 6:

GENERATION ALPHA (GEN ALPHA)

Understanding the youngest generation in the Workplace

Gen Alpha, born between 2013 and 2025, is the youngest generation
to enter the Workforce. While it may be some time before they
begin their professional careers, employers need to understand the
characteristics and expectations of this generation to engage and
retain them in the future effectively. As digital natives, Gen Alpha's
relationship with technology is unique, and they are likely to have
high expectations for innovation and learning in the Workplace.
Additionally, this generation is growing up in a world where
environmental and social responsibility is increasingly important,
and employers should be prepared to address these values in the
Workplace.

The impact of technology on Gen Alpha and their expectations

One of the defining characteristics of Gen Alpha is its relationship with
technology. They were born into a world where smartphones, tablets,
and other digital devices are ubiquitous, and they are likely to have a
high level of comfort and familiarity with technology.

As a result, they may have different expectations for the use of
technology in the Workplace. Employers prioritizing innovation and
investing in emerging technologies are more likely to attract and
retain Gen Alpha employees. Additionally, providing opportunities
for continuous learning and skill development will be necessary for
engaging this generation.

Another significant value for Gen Alpha is sustainability and social
responsibility. Growing up in a world facing environmental and
social challenges, this generation will likely prioritize sustainability
and ethical practices in the Workplace. As a result, employers can

engage Gen Alpha employees by communicating their commitment to sustainability and social responsibility and offering opportunities for employee-led initiatives supporting these values. For example, companies can encourage employees to participate in environmental volunteer work or contribute to sustainability-focused projects.

Strategies for creating a culture of innovation and learning

In addition to technology and sustainability, Gen Alpha is also likely to have a strong desire for innovation and creativity in the Workplace. They are growing up in a rapidly changing world and may expect their employers to be equally dynamic and forward-thinking. As a result, employers can engage and retain Gen Alpha employees by creating a culture of innovation and learning and providing opportunities for creative problem-solving and collaboration. This can be achieved through mentorship programs, brainstorming sessions, or other initiatives encouraging employees to think outside the box and experiment with new ideas.

Addressing the desire for sustainability and social responsibility

Finally, one should remain keenly aware that Gen Alpha is still a young generation, and their characteristics and expectations may evolve as they enter the Workforce. As such, employers should prepare to adapt their strategies and practices in response to changing trends and preferences. For example, as the world becomes increasingly globalized, Gen Alpha may value international experiences and cross-cultural competence more. As a result, employers prioritizing diversity and inclusion and providing opportunities for international travel and cultural exchange will be better positioned to attract and retain Gen Alpha employees.

Gen Alpha is a unique and diverse generation with its own set of characteristics and expectations.

Employers who understand and respond to these values will better position themselves to engage and retain Gen Alpha employees.

Employers can create a positive and productive work environment for this youngest generation by prioritizing innovation, sustainability, and learning and by adapting to changing trends and preferences.

As with any age, it's worth remembering that individual employees may have unique needs and intentions. Employers should be prepared to listen and respond to these needs to create a workplace that supports and values all of its employees.

Ultimately, by investing in the future of Gen Alpha, employers can help ensure a strong and prosperous workforce for years to come.

"Generation Alpha is the generation of dreamers and doers favored by destiny to achieve greatness and reshape the world in ways we've never imagined, with their passion, intelligence, and boundless potential."

Chapter 7:

OVERCOMING GENERATIONAL CONFLICT

Familiar sources of conflict between generations

In today's Workplace, it is not uncommon to see multiple generations working side by side. However, this diversity can also lead to generational conflicts and misunderstandings.

These conflicts can arise due to different communication styles, work values, and expectations.

Strategies for creating a culture of respect and understanding

Let's explore some familiar sources of conflict between generations and provide strategies for creating a culture of respect and understanding to overcome these differences.

Different communication styles are among the most common sources of conflict between generations.

Baby Boomers, for example, tend to prefer face-to-face communication and formal language.

Millennials and Gen Z are more likely to use digital communication platforms and informal language.

This can lead to misunderstandings and misinterpretations. To overcome this, fostering open and honest communication between generations is important.

 Encouraging each generation to express their communication preferences and finding common ground can help reduce conflict.

Indeed, this next conflict surprises no one. I am speaking, of course, about differences in work values and expectations.

Addressing issues such as communication and work style differences

Baby Boomers, for example, may value hard work and long hours, while younger generations prioritize work-life balance and flexible schedules.

To overcome this, it is crucial to create a culture of respect and understanding where each generation's values are acknowledged and appreciated.

Leaders can help by finding ways to balance the needs of each generation, such as offering flexible work arrangements or recognizing different types of work contributions. Employers can foster a more inclusive workplace.

A singularly effective strategy for overcoming generational conflict is to focus on the strengths of each generation. For example, Baby Boomers are often seen as reliable and experienced, while Millennials and Gen Z are known for their technological expertise and adaptability.

Great leaders will leverage these generational strengths and create opportunities for collaboration and mentorship, fostering a culture of learning and development that benefits all generations.

How to leverage the strengths of each generation

Of growing popularity is the offering of training and education on generational differences. These courses can help each generation better understand their colleagues' values and expectations and develop strategies for working together more effectively.

Leaders that encourage open dialogue and understanding can reduce the potential for generational conflict and create a more cohesive and productive workplace.

Work Style Issues Are Real.

Work style issues are the hush-water-cooler conversations everyone has, but no one addresses. Leaders wishing to overcome generational conflict should address work style differences. Baby

Boomers, for example, may prefer a more structured and hierarchical work environment, while younger generations may prefer a more collaborative and open approach.

By finding ways to balance these differences, such as offering different types of workspaces or allowing for more autonomy and decision-making, employers can create a more inclusive workplace that accommodates the needs of each generation.

It's Not Just the Office.

Generational conflict is not limited to the Workplace. As society becomes increasingly diverse, fostering a culture of respect and understanding in all areas of life is important. This includes family relationships, community organizations, and social groups. Recognizing and celebrating the differences between generations can create a more harmonious and accepting society for all.

The biggest struggle I am presented with during speeches and meetings is that the newer generations don't want to or don't care about the sacrifices made by previous generations.

This may be part truth and part failure to understand generational thought patterns. Still, the single best way to get everyone aligned is a mutual culture of respect and understanding, open communication, and recognition of the strengths of each generation.

Ultimately, we can create a more harmonious and accepting society for all by recognizing and celebrating generational differences.

"By recognizing and respecting the unique strengths and perspectives of each generation, we can bridge the gap of generational differences and build a world where collaboration, empathy, and understanding are the keys to success and harmony."

Chapter 8:

MANAGING MULTI-GENERATIONAL TEAMS

Managing Multi-generational Teams: A How-To Guide

This chapter is likely the reason you acquired this primer.

In today's connected world, disconnected generations are each seeking to understand how to find common ground.

Multi-generational teams are becoming increasingly common in today's Workforce. Baby Boomers delay retirement, Gen Xers take on leadership roles, Millennials and Gen Zers enter the Workforce, and Gen Alpha prepares to join soon.

While there are many benefits to having a team that spans multiple generations, some unique challenges must be addressed to ensure that everyone can work together effectively.

Let's explore some tips on managing multi-generational teams and creating a culture of collaboration and teamwork.

The Benefits and Challenges of Multi-generational Teams

While we all know that multi-generational teams bring a diverse range of perspectives, experiences, and skills to the table, each of us is keenly aware of the challenges leaders face to keep teams focused on the project itself and not the differences each generational member adds.

You must communicate effectively: Say it with words, memos, texts, video calls, ad naseum, but keep saying it if you lead a multi-generational team.

We can collectively agree that each generation has unique strengths and weaknesses. However, leveraging this uniqueness to create a high-performing team is quite possible.

For example, Baby Boomers often have a wealth of experience and institutional knowledge that can be invaluable to younger team members. At the same time, Millennials and Gen Zers may be more tech-savvy and innovative.

Anyone managing a team will be met with the first hurdle of communication. Each generation has its preferred communication style: face-to-face, phone calls, email, or instant messaging. Additionally, each generation may have its own set of jargon and acronyms that could be clearer or, to be blunt, confusing to others. This can be the team's first breaking point, leading to misunderstandings and a lack of cohesion.

Which Leaderships Style should you adopt?

Challenge your leadership style and question its effectiveness. Each generation has different expectations regarding Leadership, whether a more hierarchical or collaborative approach. This diversity in expectations instantly creates tension between team members and makes it difficult for everyone to work together effectively.

Adopt a malleable leadership style for each team member but maintains your authority to move the project, process, or company forward.

Create a Culture of Collaboration and Teamwork

One must intentionally create a culture of collaboration and teamwork to overcome the challenges of managing a multi-generational team. This starts with setting clear expectations for how team members communicate and work together. For example, you may establish guidelines for how often team members should check in with each other, what tools they should use to communicate, and how they should share information.

Each generation has its values, beliefs, and work styles, and it's essential to acknowledge and respect these differences. One can achieve this through team-building activities, cross-generational mentoring, and other initiatives encouraging team members to get to know each other better.

Addressing Issues Such as Communication and Leadership Style Differences

A leader must always be aware and recognize the differences in communication styles between generations to address communication barriers in multi-generational teams. For example, Baby Boomers prefer face-to-face communication, while Millennials and Gen Z prefer digital communication. To accommodate these differences, leaders should encourage team members to communicate most comfortably while promoting the use of multiple communication channels to ensure everyone is on the same page.

An Autocratic Leadership Style is Extinct

Autocratic leaders typically make choices based on their ideas and judgments and rarely accept advice from followers.

This fading style of Leadership creates tension in multi-generational teams. To address this issue, leaders should adopt a flexible leadership style that can adapt to the needs and preferences of each generation. For example, they may adopt a more hands-on approach with Baby Boomers while giving Millennials and Gen Z more autonomy and freedom to innovate.

Strategies for Maximizing Productivity and Creativity

To maximize productivity and creativity in multi-generational teams, seek to leverage the strengths of each generation. For example, Baby Boomers may excel at mentoring and coaching, while Millennials and Gen Z may bring fresh ideas and technological expertise. In addition, leaders should encourage cross-generational collaboration and knowledge sharing and provide opportunities for team members to learn from each other's strengths.

Yes, the Trophy Matters.

A much-used joke about different age groups is that subsequent generations got a trophy just for showing up. Well, truth be told, trophies Matter. Trophy, in this case, refers to recognition, medals, and rewards. Leaders should recognize and reward the contributions of each team member, regardless of age or experience. This can build trust and respect between team members and encourage a culture of collaboration and teamwork.

Find Your Groove

Changing a well-curated and learned leadership style is a challenging thing to do. But leading or managing a multi-generational team will stretch your skillset faster and more often than anything you have done in your professional career.

Yes, it can be challenging. Admittedly, it can feel awkward and untested, but those seeking to lead across generations should often pause, do a gravity pull assessment and "read the room" for signals.

To create a culture of collaboration and teamwork, leaders must start within themselves and focus on amending communication styles and challenging self-beliefs and generational stereotypes.

Leaders who focus on these things will be rewarded with high-functioning teams, maximized productivity, and inspirational creativity unmatched by those failing to adapt.

"Leading a multi-generational team takes discipline, understanding, and an unwavering commitment to fostering a culture of respect, collaboration, and growth, where every generation can leverage their unique strengths and perspectives to achieve collective success."

Chapter 9:

CREATING THE RIGHT CULTURE

Creating a Culture of Inclusion: A How-To Guide

Diversity and inclusion have become increasingly important topics in today's Workplace. A diverse workforce brings a variety of perspectives, experiences, and ideas that can lead to greater innovation and creativity. However, more than simply having a diverse team is required; it is crucial to create a culture of inclusion that values and supports diversity. This article will provide a how-to guide on creating a culture of inclusion in the Workplace.

The Importance of Diversity and Inclusion in the Workplace

Diversity and inclusion are essential for any workplace that wants to succeed in today's global market. A diverse workforce can bring various perspectives and ideas to the table that can help companies innovate and improve their products and services. In addition, a culture of inclusion can help to improve employee engagement and retention, leading to a more productive and happy workforce.

Creating a Culture that Values and Supports Diversity

Creating a culture that values and supports diversity is crucial for creating an inclusive workplace. This involves setting a tone from the top that emphasizes the importance of diversity and inclusion. In addition, leaders must model inclusive behavior and hold themselves and their teams accountable for creating a culture that values and supports variety.

To create a culture that values and supports diversity, organizations should also take steps to promote diversity at all levels of the organization. This includes creating a diverse pipeline for leadership positions and ensuring that various candidates have equal opportunities for advancement. In addition, organizations should also invest in diversity and inclusion training for all employees to help them understand the importance of diversity and how to work effectively with people from different backgrounds.

Addressing Issues Such as Unconscious Bias and Microaggressions

Even with the best intentions, unconscious bias and microaggressions can still occur in the Workplace. These can create an environment that is hostile to people from diverse backgrounds and undermines efforts to develop a culture of inclusion. Therefore, it is vital to address these issues head-on and create an environment where all employees feel safe and valued.

One way to address unconscious bias and microaggressions are to provide training for all employees on these topics. Training can help employees recognize their biases and understand how they can contribute to a more inclusive workplace. Additionally, organizations can create channels for employees to report incidents of bias or microaggressions and have a straightforward process for addressing these incidents.

Strategies for Recruiting and Retaining a Diverse Workforce

Recruiting and retaining a diverse workforce is essential for creating a culture of inclusion. Therefore, organizations must be intentional in their efforts to attract various candidates and create an environment where they feel valued and supported.

One strategy for recruiting a diverse workforce is to partner with organizations that serve diverse communities. Engaging with these outside organizations can assist with reaching a wider pool of candidates and demonstrate commitment to diversity and inclusion.

 Additionally, organizations should ensure that their recruitment processes are free from bias and that diverse candidates have equal opportunities for consideration.

Retaining a diverse workforce requires creating an environment where all employees feel valued and supported. This includes providing opportunities for professional development and growth, creating a culture of open communication and feedback, and ensuring that all employees feel included in decision-making processes.

In conclusion, creating a culture of inclusion is essential for any organization that wants to succeed in today's global market. It requires a commitment from Leadership to model inclusive behavior and hold teams accountable for creating a culture that values and supports diversity. Addressing issues such as unconscious bias and microaggressions is also essential, as is implementing strategies for recruiting and retaining a diverse workforce. By following these guidelines, organizations can create an environment where all employees feel valued and supported, leading to more significant innovation, creativity, and success.

"To create a culture that values and supports diversity, we must embrace inclusivity, celebrate differences, and empower individuals to bring their whole selves to work, where every voice is heard, every perspective is respected, and every idea is welcomed with open arms."

Chapter 10:

THE FUTURE OF THE MULTI-GENERATIONAL WORKPLACE

The future of work is constantly evolving and changing with the times, and demographic changes are significantly impacting the Modern Workplace. Therefore, to prepare for the next generations for work, there exists a need for commitment first to understand the changes that are occurring in the Workforce.

The first demographic change that is impacting the Workplace is the aging of the baby boomer generation. As baby boomers retire, companies face a talent gap and a need for more experienced workers. This gap is being filled by members of younger generations, such as millennials and Gen Z, who are bringing their unique perspectives and values to the Workforce.

Another major demographic change is the increasing diversity of the Workforce. As more and more people from different backgrounds and cultures enter the Workforce, companies must adapt to create a culture of inclusion that values and supports diversity.

How to prepare for the future of work

To prepare for the future of work, companies must embrace change and create a culture of adaptability and innovation. Being open to new ideas, and technologies, willing to experiment and take risks.

One of the most significant changes in the future of work is the rise of automation and the increasing use of technology in the Workplace. It is leading to concerns about job loss and the need for workers to develop new skills to remain competitive in the Workforce.

To prepare for this shift, companies must invest in training and development programs that help employees acquire the skills they need to succeed in the new economy. A process that should admittedly include both technical skills, such as data analysis and programming, as well as soft skills, such as communication and collaboration.

Addressing issues such as automation and remote work

The continued march towards universal adoption of remote work and telecommuting, accelerated by Covie-19 pandemic, is forcing many companies to shift mindsets.

To prepare for this shift, companies must invest in the technology and infrastructure to support remote work, such as video conferencing software, collaboration tools, and secure remote access to company systems. They must also develop policies and procedures that support remote work, such as flexible work hours and clear expectations for communication and productivity.

Discussing the impact of demographic changes on the Workplace

To create a culture of collaboration and innovation in the future of work, companies must also address issues such as communication and leadership style differences. Accomplishing this means creating a work environment that values open communication, feedback, and collaboration and encourages employees to share their ideas and perspectives.

Strategies for creating a culture of adaptability and innovation

As we wrap this chapter up on some predictions of the future or work, I implore you that companies must recognize the importance of work-life balance and the need for employees to have a sense of purpose and meaning in their work.

A wonderful corporate opportunity exists here by offering & providing opportunities for employees to pursue their passions, and interests by creating a culture that values social responsibility and community involvement.

I submit to you that, the future of the multi-generational Workplace is rapidly changing, and companies must be prepared to adapt and innovate to thrive.

By embracing diversity and inclusion, investing in training and development, and creating a culture of collaboration and innovation, companies can create a workplace that is both productive and fulfilling for all employees.

"The future of automation and the workplace is a world where humans and machines work in perfect harmony, where technology enhances human potential, and where creativity, innovation, and empathy are the defining factors of success, ushering in a new era of prosperity, progress, and limitless possibilities."

EPILOGUE.

The future of a multi-generational workforce will likely see even more diversity with the emergence of new generations and technological advancements. Here are some potential concepts and questions to consider:

1. Intergenerational mentorship: As the Workforce becomes more diverse, mentorship programs that pair older and younger employees can help to transfer knowledge and skills between generations. How can organizations facilitate these mentorship programs and ensure they are effective?

2. Remote work: The COVID-19 pandemic has accelerated the trend toward remote work, and many employees will likely continue to work remotely. How can organizations ensure that remote work is inclusive of all generations and that younger employees receive the support and training they need to succeed in a virtual environment?

3. Collaboration tools: With the rise of collaboration tools such as Slack and Zoom, employees of all ages can work together more efficiently. However, these tools can also be overwhelming and confusing for older workers who are less comfortable with technology. How can organizations ensure that these tools are accessible to all employees, regardless of their age or technological skills?

4. Flexible work arrangements: As younger generations prioritize work-life balance and older workers delay retirement; organizations must offer more flexible work arrangements to accommodate their employees. How can organizations balance the needs and preferences of different generations while still ensuring productivity and meeting business goals?

5. Diversity and inclusion: As the Workforce becomes more diverse, organizations must prioritize diversity and inclusion initiatives. How can organizations ensure that they are recruiting, retaining, and promoting employees from all backgrounds and that their workplace culture is inclusive and welcoming to all?

In summary, a multi-generational workforce will be shaped by technological advancements, demographic changes, and the evolving needs and preferences of employees. Organizations that can adapt to these changes and create a culture of inclusivity, flexibility, and innovation will be well-positioned for success in the years ahead.

The multi-generational Workforce is a diverse and dynamic entity that brings unique perspectives, values, and challenges to the Workplace.

Each generation has its strengths and experiences that, when leveraged effectively, can drive innovation and productivity.

To create a culture of respect, understanding, and inclusion, addressing issues such as communication, leadership styles, and work-life balance is essential while valuing and supporting diversity. In addition, preparing for the future of work requires adaptability, a willingness to embrace change, and an understanding of the impact of demographic changes, automation, and remote work.

Let's face it; the multi-generational Workforce is like a family dinner: everyone has opinions, values, and quirks, and sometimes it feels like you speak different languages. But just like at the dinner table, we've got to find a way to work together if we want to enjoy a successful meal er, Workplace.

Boomers, Gen Xers, Millennials, Gen Zs, and even the little Alphas all bring something unique to the table (pun intended), and we've got to learn how to appreciate each other's strengths and experiences. And boy, do we have some differences - from communication styles to work-life balance to our love/hate relationship with technology.

But fear not, coworkers! With a bit of understanding and some strategy, we can create a workplace where everyone feels respected, valued, and productive. We can break down those generational barriers and build a culture of collaboration and innovation. And hey, maybe we'll even learn to appreciate each other's music and fashion choices (looking at you, Gen X).

So let's grab a seat at the table and dig in (but don't forget to pass the potatoes to the Boomers first). It may not always be easy, but creating a multi-generational workplace that's a recipe for success will be worth it.

"To prepare for the future of the workplace, all generations must embrace lifelong learning, stay curious, and remain adaptable, where the ability to learn, unlearn, and relearn is the most valuable skill, and collaboration, empathy, and innovation are the keys to thriving in a world of constant change."

ABOUT JEFF ARNOLD

Jeff has been called a Thought Leader and Global Ambassador for Leadership and Multi-Generational Communication Styles. This pleases his mother and greatly surprises his wife.

He writes and speaks on Leadership, Management, Technology, Venture Capital and his favorite of subjects, the infusion of AI into Insurance.

Jeff is the author of nine books, with five of them holding the coveted "Best Seller or Number 1 ranking" His books and articles have been published in multiple countries and are highly read in The Americas and Europe.

Jeff loves to speak to anyone about his beloved industry, in a way that is engaging to those who wouldn't normally think it so.

He often speaks in executive retreats, small conference rooms, large conventions, company off-sites, impromptu Zoom calls, and to the field mice behind his desert home.

To learn more:

Personal Website: www.jeffarnold.com

Scan to connect on LINKEDIN:

LinkedIn Profile: www.linkedin.com/in/rjefferyarnold/

Other Books by Jeff are Available on Amazon

Scan for Amazon Author Page

**Scan to Buy Leaders Tip Sheets
for Difficult Conversations.**

Made in the USA
Monee, IL
23 August 2024